This book is for my students, who over
the years keep asking for my bag of
tricks. I hope these 101 projects help
to show what it takes to create magic.

LandArc
W. Garett Carlson
101 Special Gardens

Starting Out

Time flies, as they say. One day you are eight and the next you are over the hill. People always ask me what I do and how I got started. Well, first I tell them I am a gardener. I got started because I grew up with two alcoholic parents. My mom was Norwegian and my dad was a Swede. Not a good combination to begin with. Add alcohol to that and you get World War 3.

My solution to the problem was to stay out of the house as much as possible. It all started at about the age of eight. I began to take care of our yard, you know rake the leaves, mow the grass, etc. This was something I enjoyed and it got me out of the house. By the end of the summer my neighbor asked if I would take care of his yard as well. He was willing to pay me a dollar for the front and a dollar for the back. Sounded good to me!

After a few months a few more neighbors hired me as well. I was getting rich! By the time I was fourteen I was taking care of half the block. By this time I had replaced my push mower with a gas front throw—very professional!

When I was ten, one of my neighbors sent a letter to a well known landscape architect named Sid Galper. He was quite popular. He was published in *Home Magazine* almost every week. He was the first person to help guide me into the profession of landscape architecture. He sent me a personal letter telling me what classes I should take in high school and which colleges to go to for a degree.

After high school, I went to Cal Poly Pomona and majored in Landscape Architecture. When I entered, there were 250 students and by the time I graduated, there were only 35 of us left. Needless to say, it was not easy.

Each summer I worked for different nurseries, landscape contractors, tree trimmers and architects to gain an overall experience in the field.

One of the first people that I worked for was an architect in Glendale, Arthur Barton. I met him when I was 15, he was my sponsor when I became an Eagle Scout. While I was in high school I was able to work in his office part time. I did various things in the office such as helping with surveys, printing drawings and taking his wife to the doctor. It was a job and I guess you learn as you go. I think he paid me $2.50 an hour.

During college I worked with a few different architects. One office that I liked a lot was Jones and Peterson in Anaheim. They were a small firm with about 6 to 8 people. I liked this size because it allowed you do different things. In larger firms you can get stuck in one cubbyhole doing the one thing you do best. When I graduated in 1973, I was offered jobs in several large offices—EDAW in Newport Beach and SWA in San Francisco which were both large firms with over 100 people and several offices around the country. Too big and it didn't feel right—my friends thought I was crazy. This was the start of my search.

At the time I was working for a young architect, Gregg Toland, and it was just the two of us, which was great. He was fun and easy to work for. During this time I would go to different landscape projects to get a feel. I was not sure what I was looking for but hoped I would recognize it when I saw it. There are a lot of great projects out there done by big name architects. Visually these were great, but they were all lacking something.

I found out what this was when I stumbled onto an amazing project in Fox Hills. It was a Ring Brothers apartment complex with over 200 units. I had never seen anything like it. For an apartment complex it looked like a 5-star resort. This was the feeling I was looking for. It made the hair on my arms stand up. It was pure magic.

When I asked who the designer was I was told that it was a man named Phil Shipley.It turns out that he had just retired. I couldn't believe it. The strange part was that Gregg actually knew Phil. He also told me

that Phil was really the PR person—even though it was his firm, the real designer was an old guy by the name of Dudley Trudgett.

So I started to research Dudley. Not easy, since he was a bit of a hermit and Phil kept him in the back room so everyone would think that he was really the genius. When Phil retired he left Dudley high and dry. Since no one really knew who he was he had very little work and was sharing a small office with an architect by the name of Ellis Reeveness.

My first encounter with Dudley was on a Saturday at his office in West Los Angeles. My intention was to check out the office and come back on Monday to hit him up for a job. As I walked into a small courtyard of one story offices surrounding a huge Sycamore tree, I found him working at his desk. He was the only one there—I had a feeling he was my guy. As I was turning to leave he opened the window and asked if I was lost. I told him I was looking for Dudley Trudgett. He said, "That's me, what do you want?" I told him that

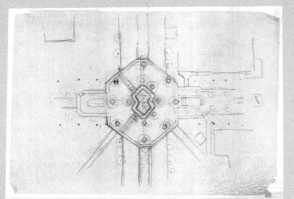
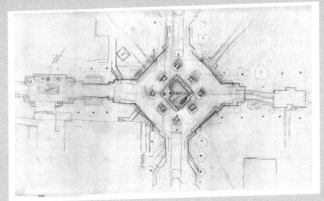

I needed to talk with him for a few minutes. He said he was busy and I should come back another time. I said ok and proceeded to leave when he again asked what I wanted. I told him that I was going to work for him but we should talk first. He laughed and as he was closing the window told me to go away. Assuming that I had blown my chance, the only thing I could think of was to say, "I will be back" although I figured this would never happen. And I left.

At this time I was asked by Jones and Peterson, the same firm that I had worked for in college, to take a job in the San Francisco Bay Area—a very nice offer that would have changed the course of my life.

Before saying yes, I thought I should give Dudley one more try. So, I went back on a Saturday as before hoping to find him alone once again. As I walked into the courtyard he saw me, got up and opened the glass door! A big improvement from the last visit. As I walked in he said to me, "What took you so long?" I was hired! It turned out that he was the mentor I was looking for. I asked him if he wanted to see some of my stuff but he said, "No. You have learned everything wrong and I need to retrain you."

And so it started. For the next five years I had to forget what I learned and learn to think in a new way. I learned how to find the magic, how to design for a feeling instead of a look and how to make a space feel as though it had been there forever.

This opened a door to another world. It turns out that he was the thing I was looking for and I was the person he needed to train. I sometimes wonder about the universe and think, "who is really in charge?"

These rough sketches are some of Dudley's courtyard designs for USC which show various solutions for the same space. This is a very important part of the design process that Dudley taught me. There are many solutions to a problem, some simple, some crazy—some more and some less expensive. The whole idea is to explore the options.

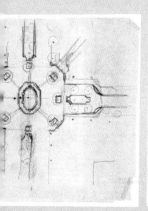
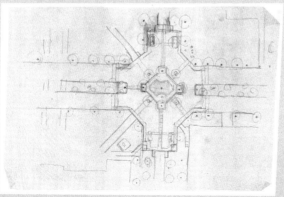
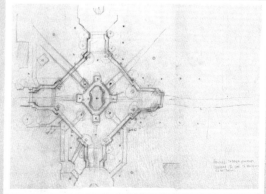

Working with Dudley

Warner Woods and Warner Village were the first large projects that I worked on with Dudley—several hundred units with lakes, streams, meandering walks and heavy landscaping. We sited all the buildings, laid out the roads and designed all the grading. The buildings were set at different angles and different elevations making the entire space feel much larger. Architects and engineers tend to lay buildings out in a formal grid pattern thus making the whole space feel smaller. If a space is designed correctly it will feel ten times larger, if not it will feel smaller. This is a key factor in great site design. I'll talk more about this later—it has everything to do with creating primary and secondary spaces.

Working with Dudley was quite a unique experience. He did not have any office hours or dress codes or really anything that a normal office had. You had work and you did your job. My job was to draw up his design sketches into working drawings that could go out to bid. His sketches were very rough but very accurate at the same time. If you looked at them you would wonder if they weren't really Egyptian hieroglyphics.

After a few months I got the hang of it and my drawing got much faster. I would always do my best to make the drawings look as good as possible. Dudley would laugh at me and say that the drawings were only a guide to get the job done and it was important to spend more time on the design and less on draw-ings. He was right of course, and this is what I believe now. Many architects spend more time on fancy drawings and graphics and less time on the design process Dudley's approach was just the opposite.

When I finish a project, I quite often hear a client say, "Wow, I had no idea." Usually that's a good thing. The drawings are important for bidding and construction, so they need to be accurate not fancy. As Dudley taught me, I do minimal drawings that are simple and easy to read.

Drawings are for the benefit of the contractor, since they are the ones doing the work. Design and installation are the most important elements of a project. Dudley and I spent a lot of time in the field—from the grading and drainage to the hard-scape layout then on to the planting and lighting. A fun part of the job was going to the nurseries to choose the specimen plant material. When the plants arrived to the job we would be there to spot and adjust in the field. You must remember that the drawing is only a guide. In the field you need to adjust everything for that perfect fit.

To get the magic you need to spend the time. Good design can be made 30% better by spending the time in the field. This does not happen much any-more—it's become an old-school way of doing things. You can't do as much work or make as much money doing it this way.

R. Dudley Trudgett in India
© *UC Berkeley Environmental Design Archives Collection*

14

Dudley did not care that much about the money—he cared more about the outcome of the work. Quite often he would donate part of his fee to buy more trees and half the time forget to bill the client. When I would ask to get paid he very often would say, "let's not talk about that now." I think I lived on about $300 a month. But I have to tell you a secret. Dudley would rent part of his house out to UCLA students. He believed that having young people around kept him young. I was able to rent a room for $50 a month, which I rarely paid, so it all worked out. The good part was I was able to spend more time with him talking about design, especially about the philosophy behind the design.

Dudley's design philosophy was unique. He believed that the site itself was the most important element and that everything should fit into that space and not dominate it. This is where I learned about primary and secondary space.

Most architects today will focus their design around the house or pool or fire pit, etc. which kills the space. These elements should be secondary not primary. When the job is finished it should look as if it's been there forever and was never designed. Everything should blend together. This is harder than it sounds.

When Dudley was teaching me his design process he would have me create ten different design solutions for the space. The idea behind this was to give the client options to choose from. This would get them involved in the design and would allow interesting combinations to come together. Coming up with different solutions expands your brain and allows you to better solve problems. Creativity is flexibility.

What creates the magic? It's all about energy. And what creates the energy? When I first saw one of Dudley's jobs, it was the energy I felt, not the look. There was minimal hardscape, maximum landscape and a ton of trees—I mean a whole forest of trees. I wondered how he did this.

I learned later that there is an art to this kind of heavy landscape. The trees are the key. Dudley would say that trees make people happy. The trees have the most energy so the more trees the better.

Do you know that five trees planted close together won't get any bigger than one tree planted in that same spot? A tree will adapt to the space where it's planted. I have pictures taken of trees planted in tight spaces after 60 years that are doing fine. Some trees may lift a sidewalk but rarely do damage to walls or structures. It's cheaper to fix a sidewalk than remove a tree. An older tree is worth a lot more than a sidewalk—fix the sidewalk!

Trees also produce oxygen plus shade and habitat for animals. I design my gardens to have 1/3 hardscape and 2/3 landscape. With the trees, I design for 1/3 deciduous and 2/3 evergreen. This allows for more sunlight in the winter and a change of season. There is an art to how you mix different trees together and Dudley was a master at this.

The Early Years

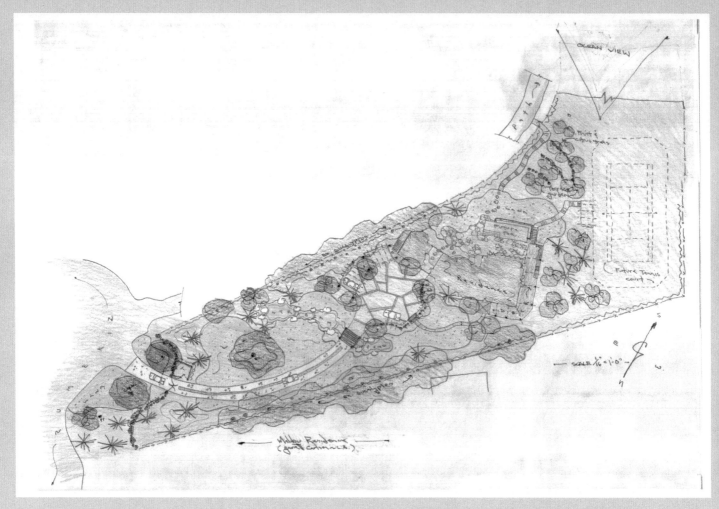

Final sketch for Grant Feury Residence

After working with Dudley for a few years, I started doing a few projects on my own. One of the very first ones was for the mother of a friend of mine. It was a small garden and my fee was $50, a dinner and a book on Maxfield Parrish. The one dinner turned into many. The dinner idea was so good that it became part of my fee for many years to come.

Everyone has a big break at some point in their career. Mine came rather early—somewhere around 1975. I was walking down the street in Santa Monica when a beautiful woman came out of a store carrying several bags and knocked me down. After she apologized, she asked me what I did. When I told her that I was a landscape architect, she smiled and said, "just the person I could use." She and her husband were building a house in Malibu and some of the existing trees on the 3-acre property were not doing well. She asked if I would come and take a look. I said, "Sure, anytime. How about now?" OK. So off we went in her car to Zumirez Canyon.

It was an empty lot with a beautiful view of the ocean. There were several old Eucalyptus trees that were stressed due to the drought at the time. They just needed water and would be fine. Then she pulled a set of architectural plans out of the trunk of her car.

The plan showed a large house with a tennis court in front. Once you squeezed by the tennis court, you came to a large motor court and then a large two-story house. There was no view of the ocean until you entered the house and even then the first thing you saw was a massive fireplace—a very bad site plan to say the least. I suggested moving the tennis court behind the house and down the slope. This would create the chance to have a beautiful winding entry perhaps with a lake and a bridge. Who wants to look at a tennis court? By putting it down the back slope, it would disappear, keeping the ocean view. She asked if I would be willing to help them with the design.

This was my first big job and I was very excited. I totally re-designed the site and modified the house plan to better fit the site. I made the motor court more natural to fit into the landscape and moved the tennis court to the back hillside. I also split the house so when you entered the motor court you got a shot of the ocean. All in all a very nice and totally natural design. The house was wood and glass so it all fit.

I was happy, the clients were happy. The architect, Peter Choate, was pissed! Really pissed! My theory is that if someone has a good idea, use it. I was young and had a lot to learn. The clients asked Peter to change his drawings to fit mine. He was only to work on the house and I was in charge of the garden. When the job finished it turned out really great. It was written up in several magazines and got a lot of press. Peter took credit for everything and my name was never mentioned. We never worked together again, however, I do think he became aware of how important site design is.

My client here was Lee Grant, a beautiful actress and her husband, Joe Feury.

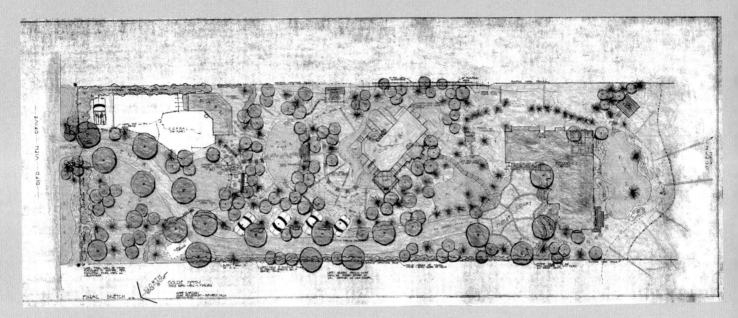

Final sketch for Hawn Hudson Residence

Lee was a good friend of Goldie Hawn and she was also building a house at the same time with her then husband Bill Hudson.

This was my second big job which then led to many more. One of the things I remember about that job was tagging trees with Goldie. One day in Anaheim we stopped for lunch. While waiting in line, everyone was whispering wondering if that was really Goldie. One little girl about 10 years old came up to her and asked if she was really Goldie Hawn. Goldie got down on her knees and talked with that girl about Girl Scouts and who knows what else. That brave little girl was in heaven. At this time Goldie just had a baby, Kate Hudson. I remember carrying her around in my arms while walking with Goldie on the job site. I love to tell people that I have had Kate Hudson in my arms several times.

Several years later I did another house for Goldie and Kurt Russell. We went tagging trees for this house as well. To me this is an important part of the project.

20

Trees are very personal and should be hand-picked together with the client and the architect, if possible. Depending on what we found on these outings and what the client liked, the plan would often be adjusted accordingly. Having a smaller office allowed me to be more hands-on taking things to a higher level.

At this point in my career I was living in a small studio about 300 sq. ft. and sleeping on my roof. The roof was flat and I turned it into a garden which became my bedroom, giving me more room downstairs to work. My rent was $150 a month, I owned two pairs of pants, three white shirts, and an old car. It was perfect! I think several clients actually hired me because I was this crazy guy who slept on his roof.

Don and Nancy Dick were building a house in Westlake Village. The architect-builder designed the house and site. When I got there the pool had just been gunited. The builder was planning on paving the whole backyard and hanging a large wood deck off the backside of the pool. The entire back slope was to be unused. Wasted space!

What I proposed was to swap out the hardscape for landscape and reverse the primary and secondary spaces. By placing the elements throughout the site rather than dominating the site it would make the property feel bigger and give it a much better flow. The great views they had would be killed by a deck and handrail. Everyone on the job told Don that I did not know what I was doing and should be fired.

Don on the other hand was a risk taker and believed in me so he gave me a chance. We spent $250,000 on the total landscape which was a lot of money at that time, 1975. It worked and I became a part of the family. A few years later Don bought me a condominium in Moorpark for $67,000.

At the time I was 28 years old and living in my small studio and still sleeping on my roof. I never really wanted to own anything and was into having a simple life. Don felt that I needed to join the real world. He brought me to his bank and told the president to get me set up and help me when needed. This got me started and helped me get to where I am today. He was a major factor in my life. He died six months later in a plane crash. Nancy stills lives in the same house today and I have watched the kids grow up and become adults with their own kids. Time flies!

Another project of my early career was for a beautiful artist by the name of Sonia Weiss. She came to me one day for my advice about buying a house in the Hollywood Hills. It was a John Barrymore house built in 1928. The house was on Outpost Drive which was a busy street that connected Hollywood to the valley.

The house was priced at $180,00. I felt it had potential and told her to buy it. The key to make the house work was to get rid of the noise. There is always a key to unlock the magic and make a project work. In this case it was a wall. We painted the wall and house to look more Spanish and added a couple of Toltec figures at the entry.

This house became quite famous and later sold for over $2 million. While working on the project we both fell in love and were together for a few years. Sonia was 50 and I was 25.

This Beverly Hills residence for Karen and Marvin Finell was another early project of mine. It was a hillside property that was locked in with a lot of hardscape and very bad circulation.

By reworking the circulation pattern I was able to get the space I needed for landscape—once again pulling the design elements into a secondary position and al-lowing the landscape to become more primary. I also used brick to tie into the tile roofs in the distance—borrowed scenery as the Japanese call it. This is a very important element in design and should be used whenever possible. Quite often I will use trees that you see in the background into the foreground of the design. It's all about making the space feel bigger.

Big Decision Time

After working with Dudley for five years and starting to work on my own projects, my plan was to go back east and work for Dan Kiley. He and Dudley had been together at Harvard and was one of the Fab Four as they are called in the Landscape Architectural community. He lived in Vermont and worked primarily on the East Coast. This was a different type of design and something I wanted to learn.

The year was 1978 and I had a choice to make. I could go back east or stay here and continue working with Dudley. If I stayed, I would be able to enter the UCLA graduate program in Architecture and contine to grow my own office. The West Coast won out and I guess I was meant to stay with Dudley. I think the universe was voting as well. UCLA turned out to be a lot of fun and gave me knowledge I would use later in my career.

At this point I was still living in the small studio and sleeping on my roof. This was to be very temporary but lasted 10 years.

The good part of this was being close to Dudley, even though I was now doing more of my own projects and working with Dudley less, he would always come to visit me every night at my studio. He would walk in and pull up a chair next to my drawing table and look at what I was designing and say, "that's terrible!" I would laugh and ask him how to make it better.

Together we would make it better! The next night he would come over and say the same thing again and we would go through the process again. Dudley and I both had the same time table. Get up late and work late.

His visits to me would usually be around midnight, a good time for a break. We would spend about an hour in our debates. All of this helped reinforce my design principals and was a huge part of my training. I was very lucky to have a mentor like Dudley.

A funny story: my studio was very small so I had to be very clever in the utilization of space. I had two drawing tables, a small kitchen and bathroom and a small closet that held five hangers and my blueprint machine. When I made blueprints I would have to remove the clothes.

Quite often I would have parties on the roofW. Dudley always made it a point to pop over with his empty glass. As he would come up the stairs he would say, "Oh, do you have any wine?"

He would then promptly sit down and start drinking and take over the conversation. Usually it would be about how important gardens were and how trees made people happy. "Do you know if there were more trees in the inner cities there would be less crime and more happy people?" I think there is truth to that.

I miss Dudley and I miss sleeping on the roof. When Dudley died in 1985 I bought his house and turned it into my office. The following year I bought the studio house next door as well. I rent the main part of the house and still use the studio as I did so long ago.

29

My Career
and Bag of Tricks

Lets talk about process. When I start a project, the first step is to make a complete survey of the property showing all of the existing conditions—a measured drawing showing the buildings with doors and windows indicated, all major trees, and surrounding elements that impact the site. An accurate survey is very important for accurate design.

After meeting with the client and hearing about their needs and goals, I do a series of sketches showing various solutions for the property. These are plan view color sketches hand-drawn to scale. I usually do 4 or 5 different sketches going from simple to out-of-the-box. This gives the client some options. Then, the various elements that the client chooses are put into a final or composite sketch.

After the final sketch has been reviewed and approved by the client, a contract is then created for working drawings and field observation. There is no contract until this point. The sketch fee is separate. My reason is, if they don't like my ideas they can bail at this point—or if I have a bad feeling I can bail. No harm, no foul!

My working drawings are very simple, showing all the required work with a minimum of drawings. The more complex the project, the more detail you need to show. For instance, on most residential projects I don't include an irrigation plan. I will spec out the type of equipment that I want used and let the landscape contractor design it in the field. Quite often the landscape changes during construction so the irrigation needs to change as well. If it is a commercial job that requires an irrigation plan I have an irrigation consultant that does this for me. The most important thing is full coverage. Since the landscape contractor is responsible for the guarantee of the plant material, the right irrigation is essential.

When the job is done, I will do a walk-through to look at the coverage. A good thing to remember is that as the plant material grows, the irrigation needs to be adjusted. This is a maintenance issue. Drainage is another issue that needs to be observed. If drainage is required I will usually show catch basins in the areas needed, and make a note to adjust in the field as necessary to conform to the final grading. This is crucial. As long as you have 1% fall you are ok—if not, perhaps a sump pump is needed.

Good drawings with good notes will give you accurate bids and be a guide to get the job done. The field observation is most important. This is where you have the potential to make the design better and solve problems before they become problems. Good field observation will make the project 30% better. I lay everything out in the field with the contractor, from hardscape to planting and lighting.

A final walk-through at completion with the client is the last thing to be done. At this point, dinner comes with it hopefully.

Dorian Safan Residence
Pacific Palisades

The following is an example of the entire process, showing all of the sketches and drawings. This project was a residence in the Palisades. Steve and Jane were great to work with. Good clients become part of the team and are more invested in a good outcome.

Before

Preliminary Sketches

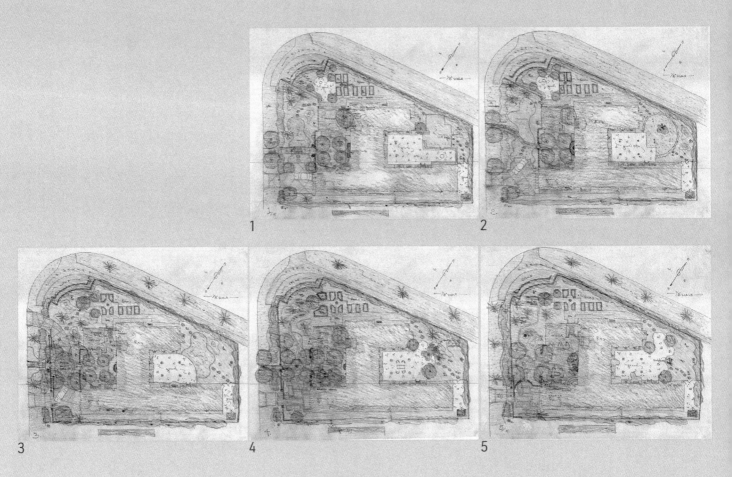

1
2
3
4
5

Final Sketch

Existing Conditions Drawing

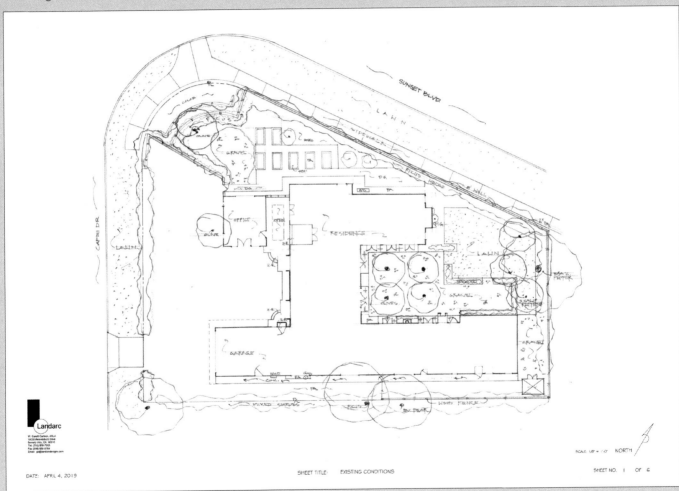

Construction Plan Drawing

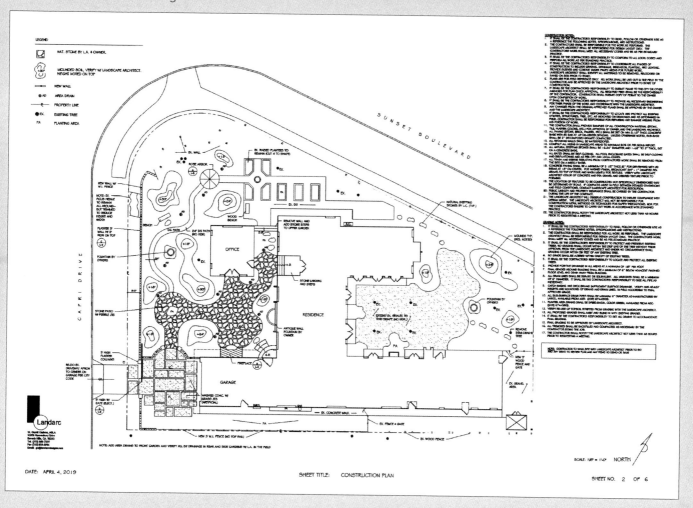

Details Plan Drawing

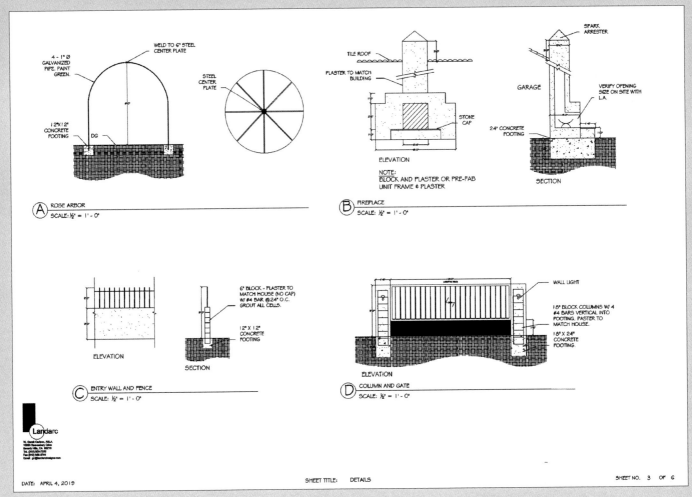

4 - 1" Ø GALVANIZED PIPE. PAINT GREEN.

WELD TO 6" STEEL CENTER PLATE

STEEL CENTER PLATE

12"X12" CONCRETE FOOTING

DG

Ⓐ ROSE ARBOR
SCALE: ½" = 1' - 0"

TILE ROOF

PLASTER TO MATCH BUILDING

STONE CAP

ELEVATION

NOTE:
BLOCK AND PLASTER OR PRE-FAB
UNIT FRAME & PLASTER

Ⓑ FIREPLACE
SCALE: ½" = 1' - 0"

SPARK ARRESTER

GARAGE

VERIFY OPENING SIZE ON SITE WITH L.A.

24" CONCRETE FOOTING

SECTION

6' BLOCK - PLASTER TO MATCH HOUSE (NO CAP) W/ #4 BAR @24" O.C. GROUT ALL CELLS.

12" X 12" CONCRETE FOOTING

ELEVATION

SECTION

Ⓒ ENTRY WALL AND FENCE
SCALE: ½" = 1' - 0"

WALL LIGHT

18" BLOCK COLUMNS W/ 4 #4 BARS VERTICAL INTO FOOTING. PLASTER TO MATCH HOUSE.

18" X 24" CONCRETE FOOTING.

ELEVATION

Ⓓ COLUMN AND GATE
SCALE: ½" = 1' - 0"

Landarc

W. David Carlson, ASLA
15000 Rensselaer Drive
Beverly Hills, CA 90210
Tel: (310) 859-2589
Fax: (310) 555-5744
Email: gm@landarcdesigns.com

Tree and Lawn Plan Drawing

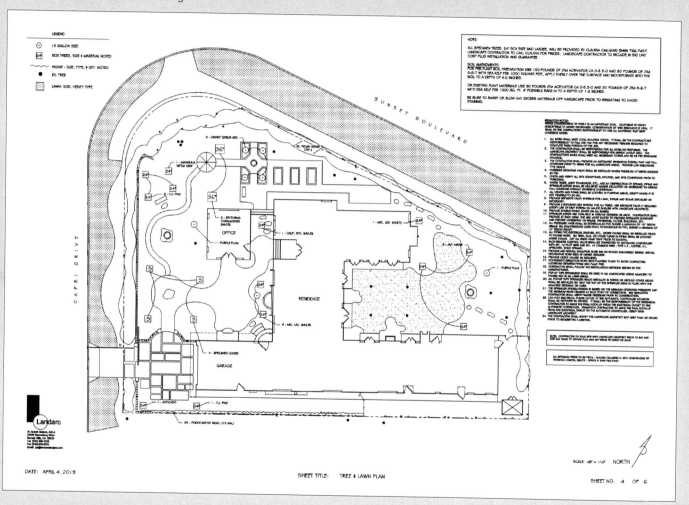

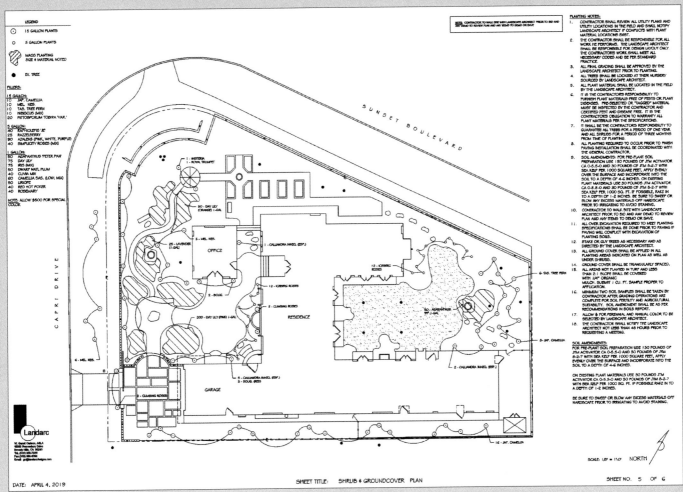

Lighting Plan Drawing

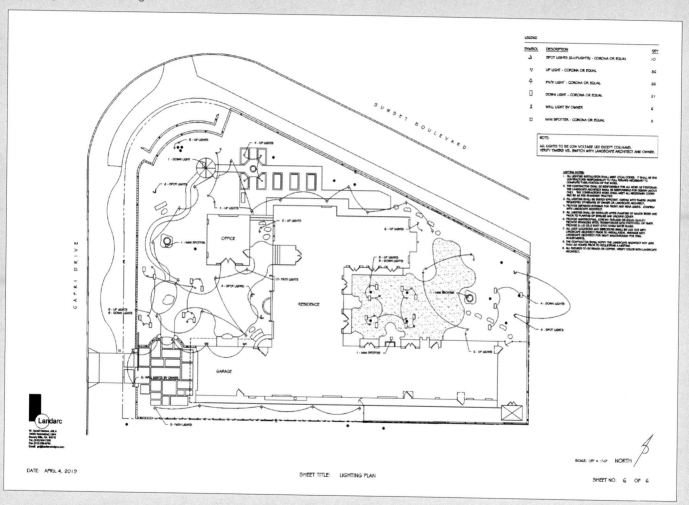

"I was representing the seller of a brand new ultra high-end modern home in Trousdale whose interiors had been designed by a well-known San Diego firm. The seller and I decided to fluff it up for photographic purposes. The design firm sent a talented associate who was accompanied by his husband, who happened to be an attorney with a passion for landscaping. I mentioned that I was having a hard time finding a landscape architect who understood traditional homes and gardens for work I wanted for my own home. Without hesitation he said that I had to find Garett Carlson although he wasn't sure if he was still working as it was rumored that he had moved out of the area.

With a little bit of digging I found Garett's website and became enthralled. I slid my laptop over to my husband and in an instant we knew that Garett was our guy.

We walked the property and Garett said something to the effect that we had a blank canvas with great potential and it could be an exciting project. We then sat down and discussed what we envisioned.

Garett came back to our home after meticulously measuring and walking the property. If I remember correctly, he found a discrepancy between the actual space and the architect's survey.

Garett then presented us with a set of different ideas. The first sketch was exactly what we asked for and we thought we were pleased. He then said "go with me on something" and we said "Sure." The second sketch gave the space a bit more movement, but was still similar to the first sketch. He had captured our attention with the improvement of the second sketch and we were interested in seeing the next one. The next two sketches departed a bit from from the first two and we were intrigued. We didn't know it at the time, but he was taking us in a totally different direction and opening us to options we hadn't imagined.

He then said, "I have one more sketch—something totally out of the box." When he unfurled the final sketch, I had a religious experience. I could not believe he could have imagined our space in a way that upended every perception I had. Without hesitation I said, "There is no choice—we have to go with this one."

While I know he played us like a fiddle, his presentation took us down a creative path that meanders as effortlessly as the walk in the park he gave us. Every day, the genius landscaping he designed for us makes our home quite special. Not a second goes by where we do not have access to our outdoor space. His work gives us pleasure every day. The transformation is as magical as the landscape architect who created it! More we cannot thank you!!!"

—Jane Dorian

101 Special Gardens

The following projects all tell a story. After teaching at UCLA for 16 years off and on, I now look at design from the student's point of view. I tell my students that every designer has a bag of tricks. The better the designer, the bigger the bag of tricks. I teach only winter quarter and take a maximum of 10 students and I do this for free. The idea is to plant a few seeds that hopefully one day will grow and allow Dudley's and my philosophy to continue.

Intimate garden design is going away, unfortunately. The small landscape firms are slowly disappearing, leaving the larger firms doing the larger projects such as parks and regional planning. I still feel that the residential garden is very important for feeding the soul.

When I started out I was very fortunate to work with very high-end architects who appreciated the value of the landscape architect. One that I respected highly was Hal Levitt. He would always bring me in at the beginning so we could develop the house and site together.

After several years of working on my own, I went back to UCLA and entered the graduate program in architecture. I was the only landscape architect out of a class of 35 architects going for their masters. When it was my turn to present they would all say "OK, let's see what the gardener has." My design concepts would always be different because I would make the structures fit into the site rather than dominate the site. This goes back to primary and secondary space and the site should always be primary whenever possible.

The main difference between architects and landscape architects is that architects learn to design in a 2-dimensional form with fixed spaces while landscape architects design in a 3-dimensional form—unlimited space.

This is the main reason why landscape architects make better site designers and should always be brought in at the beginning. Architects, such as Hal Levitt, believed this to be the best way to design.

I worked on a project for John Tunney, former United States Senator from California. He hired me to design the site first—five acres in Malibu. I created a design for the placement of all the structures, pool, roads, parking and also created a grading plan. At this point, he then hired an architect to design the buildings following my site plan. This happens rarely now.

Before

Before

First Transformation

First Transformation

Second Transformation

Second Transformation

nal Transformation

Briskman Garden
Beverly Hills

This was a garden I designed three different times, twice for Gary and Linda Briskman and the final time for the next owner. It is amazing how you can take the same space and transform it to achieve a totally different feeling. When I talk about designing for a feeling rather than a look this is a good example.

Schulman Garden

Brentwood

This was a very modern house which was designed by Conrad Buff of Buff and Hensman in Pasadena. This was the last house that Conrad designed before he died. The house was designed to have a large wall enclosing the front entry with a large parking area outside the wall.

I took the wall out and dropped the driveway down and created a park instead. My elevated entry walk was a spine that carried through the house to a pool and water element in the back. Arriving at the entry you cross over a dry lake bed and go through a grove of cottonwoods. At night the trees are up-lit, casting shadows against the stark white house—very dramatic. During the day you have great shadows and the sound of rustling leaves similar to an Aspen grove.

Sahrodian Garden

Palos Verdes

This is a beautiful house built on the bluff overlooking the ocean. The house took five years to build and sits on caissons 80 ft. deep. The feeling we were after was the Amalfi coast in Italy—and a feeling of timelessness.

Before

Barrett Garden

Beverly Hills

This was the first house I did for Rona. The pool was gunited when I was hired. I was the second designer on the job. The problem was the pool was too close to the house making the property feel small. We moved the Magnolia tree and re-shaped the pool to extend to the back of the property thus making the property feel larger. Also by getting rid of the straight lines we took away the boxiness which made a big difference.

This was the first time I re-shaped a pool and used boulders in the pool, which made it quite fun to swim. After the job finished she gave me swimming privileges. I loved it since I lived just up the canyon.

Since this project, I have done about eight more for Rona over the years. She is a very good friend and her birthday is one day after mine. I get a call every year. She is one of a very few that know my birthday!

Laskey Residence
Pacific Palisades

This was an early job of mine. The property was 13 acres with a great view of the ocean. There were a few challenges to the site. Lots of slope, water issues and a very large wall at the entry. To get rid of the wall I created an arbor covered in vines, a good trick to get rid of a tall vertical element. I created many dry creek beds to catch and direct the water and re-graded a large area of the site to create space for the pool and park. The pool had a small dock for a small row boat and I also included fish to swim with.

To my big surprise no one wanted to swim with the fish! Oh well, I thought it was a good idea at the time. This was also my first sod roof structure. The planting on the roof helps it blend into the background. Blending a space—a very important trick.

59

Thompson Residence
Beverly Hills

The architect had the motor court level with the front door. I lowered it 4 ft. and pulled it away from the house giving privacy to the house and a much better entry. In the back I also lowered the grade and added on to the terrace with a bar and bathroom underneath to service the pool. This is a very good example of why architects and landscape architects should work together from the very start.

Both Larry and Lauren were great to work for and we had great fun. One day when we went tagging trees we went in Larry's Rolls Royce. It was raining and Lauren had on high heels so we carried her through the nursery. She was very small and quite light. Claudia, my longtime tree broker, still loves to tell this story.

Beverly Hills Garden

This property was way up high in Trousdale. My client bought the lot next door so we could create a park. The luxury of space in the city is quite rare. The sound of the pond and waterfalls made a big difference.

Gilbert, my rock guy as I call him, is one of the best around. I have worked with him for over 30 years. You would never know the rocks are artificial.

Rosenberg Residence

Encino

This was a typical 70s ranch house. I did not change the house at all—just the site around it. You would never know it's the same house. We made the entry private with a small water element at the front door. This was a great place for morning coffee and watching the birds take a bath.

In the backyard we took the existing pool and added several water walls that appear to all connect to the pool. The idea was to draw your eye up the hill, which included pathways and sitting areas with great views. We also anchored the pool with an arbor and outdoor fireplace.

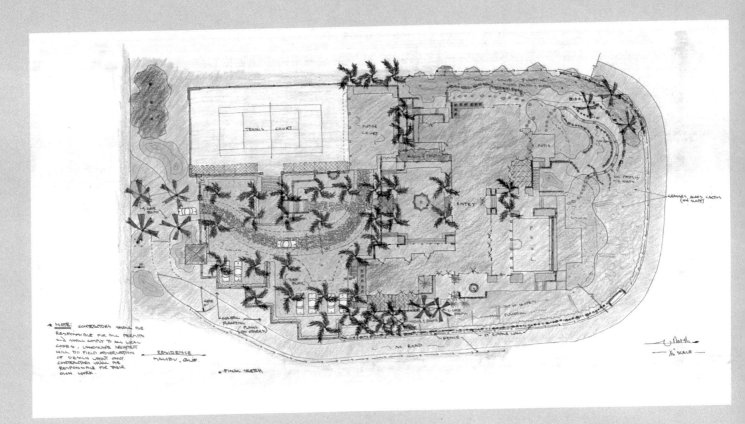

Site plan

Cher Residence

Malibu

I was the seventh landscape architect she hired. This was a challenge to say the least. The house was too big for the site and everything was out of scale. The key that made it work was a grove of palm trees. I used the date palm you see in Palm Springs—very hardy and very cheap. I used 40 of them on a grid pattern which was the impetus of the design. They were 25-30 ft. tall and instantly brought the house into scale.

Before

Braun Residence

Hollywood Hills

This was a great house up in the hills with great views and great trees. We worked the garden around the trees and views. When we were finished you would never know it was ever designed—it felt like it was always there.

The key was the curve of the pool. This allows the eye to travel through to the view beyond. The trick here is to stay away from straight lines whenever possible. This is one important way of making the space feel bigger.

Gallin Residence
Beverly Hills

Sandy Gallin was a personal business manager for people like Dolly Parton and others. He had great taste but was very hard to work for. On the first project we had a very low budget. I needed to be very creative in my design and spend money where it was most important.

One trick I used was with the paving around the pool. Instead of cut stone which cost around $40,000, I used plain concrete which I sand blasted and saw cut into a pattern and sealed with a color—$5,000, not bad.

The interesting part of this story was that Sandy sold the house to Frank Sinatra and made a tidy profit in less than one year. Sinatra loved the garden. I was now very popular with Sandy!

A year later he called me with another project. I told him I would rather become a truck driver and hung up.

71

Later that day, I got a call from his lawyer. He said that I could work directly with him rather than Sandy. There was no budget and I could do whatever I wanted. What a difference!

The big problem was that the house came right to the top of the slope, leaving no room for a terrace or pool. My solution was to build a pool in midair off the back slope with grade beams back to the house for the terrace. The pool was 70 ft. with a curve and planters hanging off the back side with specimen olive trees. The pool sat on five caissons and cost $250,000. It looked like Noah's Ark from down below.

Archie Kapp built the pool and did most of my pools throughout my career. To keep from having guard rails on the back side of the pool, I designed a knife edge to keep the view. This was written up in several magazines and was in a book of the 200 greatest pools in the world. Sandy took credit for the design. Oh well, this happens a lot. This was the pool that started all the horizon pools that you see today. The idea is not a new one and has been done before. John Lautner, a great architect, did a similar one called Silver Top in Silver Lake about 20 years earlier.

This was my last project for Sandy. We spent a little over $2 million in the garden and when the house sold it was the highest selling house in the city at that time. He made another tidy profit!

Edwards Andrews Residence
Beverly Hills

This was an interesting job since I never once met the owners. They were in Europe at the time. Blake Edward's nephew DW Owen, a friend of mine, recommended me to them and so I was hired. That Christmas I got a card from Julie Andrews telling me how much they loved the garden.

The key that made the space work was lowering the driveway by 18 inches. I ended up getting more parking with one-third less paving and room for a lot more planting. Organization of space is important.

Before

75

Supowitz Residence Japanese Garden

Encino

This property was not very large but when we finished it felt like acres. I worked with the architect to design the teahouse floating over water.

The lighting is a crucial element that can make a big difference. Lighting has come a long way with LED now becoming state-of-the-art. The way I light a garden is quite unique. The right combination of fixtures—up lights, down lights, pathway lights, lanterns, etc.—creates the mood.

Schwartz Residence

Las Vegas

There was a very busy street behind this property. The large water
wall eliminated the noise and gave
a beautiful backdrop both day and
night. It was the main focal point of
the garden.

80

Carpenter Residence

Hollywood Hills

John Carpenter was a very interesting guy—he wrote music and created movies. When he told me what he wanted, I told him to forget it. The house was not worth the cost it would take to create such a garden.

He told me "Garett, you do what you do best and let me do what I do best, and we won't talk about money!" He was good to his word. It took over two years to create this.

The 35 ft. retaining wall gave me the bathtub I needed to create the garden. We had 35 ft. by 70 ft. to work with. Archie Kapp, my pool genius, built the pool, of course.

Bergman Residence

Lake Sherwood

I had 50 acres to create a master site plan. With a long entry drive starting off with a small lake, you went through groves of trees passing a tennis court and rose garden. You then arrive at a castle-like house overlooking a natural pool and a pool house with view that goes on forever. We created 6 ft. pathways for a golf cart to take you around the property. We planted well over a thousand trees of all types including fruit and citrus plus native plants of all types as well.

Coletto Residence
Woodland Hills

This was a very simple house in a typical housing development. When we finished it felt like it belonged in Northern California rather than the San Fernando Valley. Note how the garden has now become the primary space and the pool has become secondary.

Before

Candy Residence
Mandeville Canyon

John had just bought the house next door to enlarge his property to a little over 3 acres. We tore the house down and re-graded the entire property to build a tennis court, pool and pool house. John loved trees so we planted a lot of them.

He loved the garden. There were winding pathways going through the entire property with koi ponds, waterfalls and hidden seating areas— and lots and lots of trees! John died right at the end of the project while in Mexico doing a movie and the property was sold to Mark Attanasio.

Before

87

Attanasio Residence

Mandeville Canyon

Mark told me he bought the house strictly for the garden. He tore the house down and built a much larger one. I had to work with the New York architect to make sure the garden was not compromised.

By breaking up the terraces off the house I was able to blend the house into the garden. The property has a great feel to it.

Brentwood

Malibu

Riley Residence

Brentwood and Malibu Beach House

I did two houses for Pat and Chris. The first one in Brentwood was when Pat was coach of the Lakers. I took out a pool that was in the middle of the garden and designed a new one off to one side keeping a view down the middle to a paddle tennis court. By keeping the center of the court open on both sides the eye is able to continue—a very simple trick making the space feel bigger. I also changed the front of the house which made a big difference.

Several years later I did a second house for them at the beach. The architect for the house wanted to also do the gardens. Chris insisted that I do the gardens—she believed in me. There was a tight space in the back where we terraced the hill with small walls and created an intimate sitting area with a firepit and water-wall. In the front, we created a bocce ball court and a floating walkway to the house.

Before

Ravich Garden

Pacific Palisades

This was a beautiful property over-looking the ocean—an old estate built in the 20s. While doing the garden I was asked by the owners to do a secret garden for their little girls. The space I was given was 20ft by 100ft and was used by the gardener for trash. At each end I created small wooden doors cut into stone walls that took you into another world. Winding pathways and pressure loaded stepping stones blasted you with water from topiary animals. There was a sand play area, a vegetable garden and a tea house. It was a big hit with all the kids at their school.

One day I got a call from a magazine in New York, *House and Garden*, asking to photograph it. I could never find out how they even knew about it. It was a very nice article, however.

Fishman Residence

Tarzana

We did this garden twice. The first time we enclosed the front and created more privacy and security. Years later, when grandchildren arrived, we came back and worked on the back garden. We created a kid's garden with pathways through a jungle on the back hill plus a great slide made of concrete to look like an old hollow tree. Very fast and lots of fun for kids and adults alike. Another masterpiece by Gilbert. I have to tell you that when grandkids are involved you get a much bigger budget!

Stenning Garden

Camarillo

I did the original garden 25 years ago when the house was first built. Over the years I came back to do little things. Last year I came back to create a little magic on the lower back hillside.

You enter the garden through a large wall with a portal in the middle. You walk on a small pathway past water elements and sculpted rocks through an artificial tree branch gazebo and end up at a meditation area with a small Buddah. On your way out you take another secret path and end up back in the main garden at the large koi pond.

Lola is in her 80s and going strong. The garden is a very important part of her life. We could all learn from her.

Before

Johnson Residence
Pacific Palisades

Eric Johnson hired me because my name was Carlson and according to him, since we were both Scandinavians, we should stick together. I ended up doing several more projects for them.

The key that made this one work was scale. I reduced the driveway and separated the pedestrian walk from the main drive. I put in a VertiGate since we were on a slope and did not have room to do a sliding gate. Adding olive trees on both sides of the walk gave it intimacy and great lighting options. You should always think of how the garden will work during the day and night and design accordingly. The motor court is washed concrete with artificial grass joints. We developed the back hill with grapes, fruit trees and lots of native plants, creating a great area for the grandkids to play.

Brentwood

Santa Monica

Cowan Garden

Brentwood and Santa Monica

Bob and Audrey were early clients in my career. The first house I did was a rustic house in Brentwood on a nice piece of property. We did a pool, paddle tennis court and nice terraces with interesting tiles overlooking the lower garden. In the front we did a gravel circular driveway. Bob had insisted on a circular drive because, as he put it, when he grew up if you had a circular drive at your house it meant you were rich. Well, whatever makes you happy!

Years later they sold that house and bought one closer to the beach. It had great views, however it looked down on the garage roof. To solve the problem I created a Japanese roof garden. This also tied your eye to the landscaping in the distance and made the garden feel bigger—borrowed scenery!

101

Bider Residence
Beverly Hills

This was an old property with a tennis court that took up half the garden. By taking the tennis court out, we gained 7,000 sq. ft. of garden. We moved the pool to the back of the property and created terraces with an outdoor fireplace and a great view of the garden. We also cut an opening in the back of the garage so you could exit the property through the back alley, and gained more parking at the same time.

Before

Ahdout Residence

Brentwood

Jackie and Yahya have been great friends of mine for many years. Years ago when the kids were young they came to visit me in Colorado. We all went river rafting and horse-back riding. Yahya has never forgiven me! I think if you look at him closely you might notice that he is a little bow-legged?

They have a special garden. It's Jackie's pride and joy. She has added her own special touches to make it even better.

105

Adelson Residence

Beverly Hills

This was a very small backyard with a steep hillside that came right down to the back of the house. There was a 3 ft. retaining wall with a chain-link fence on top and an ivy-covered hillside. We re-graded to cover the existing wall and ran lawn up to a level pad where we desiged the pool and patio. This was the perfect spot for the sun and the view.

Before

Delle Donne Residence

Tarzana

This was a great piece of property on a flag lot. We remodeled the pool and changed the entry drive and added some beautiful Italian pots to the garden to add color and interest.

Before

Davidman Residence

Encino

Besides the garden, we gave the house a face lift as well. We took off the wood siding and did a smooth plaster, replaced the wood sash windows with clean vinyl, cut the roof back and painted the roof trim black to match the windows. Its amazing what a little cosmetic surgery can do. Its important to look at the whole picture. In this case, the changes to the house and garden together made the difference.

Petty Residence
Malibu

A simple garden overlooking the ocean. A nice transformation.

Right after the pool was plastered and before it was filled with water, Tom's son and one of his friends went in with their skateboards. We ended up leaving it with the tracks.

Before

Poublan Residence

Encino

These were two properties that we put together. To make the back house work we designed an arbor that went over the roof covered in vines. By raising the arbor we were able to hide a good portion of the roof. This gave the appearance of a guest house behind the pool.

Before

Perkins Residence

Hollywood Hills

Tony and Berry were two of my favorite clients. Very down-to-earth and very real. Tony had a '57 T-Bird and Berry had a '57 Chevy. At that time I had a '69 Buick 225.

The house was in Laurel Canyon and Tony loved the vibe. We gave the house a little more privacy and security while keeping the rustic feel of the canyon.

Before

Before

Passman Residence

Beverly Hills

When Don and Shana bought the house 35 years ago, I designed the front and the back. They never felt that my solution for the front worked, so, only the back was done. The problem was the pool took up the entire yard and was quite a bit lower than the house. Looking down made the garden feel small. The solution was to raise the backyard up 2 ft. and move the pool to the back. This made the garden the primary space and the pool secondary. Two years ago, they came back to me to take another look at the front. I came up with the same solution as before and this time we chalked it out, they tested it and we agreed—it does work!

Before

119

Before

Payson Residence

Hollywood Hills

A very small garden on a steep hillside—most of which was paved in tile. The solution was to divide the patios with garden between. We built a floating wood deck with a redwood hot tub and a small sun patio with wood stairs down the hill to another sitting area and garden. I have a great method of creating wooden stairs down a steep slope without any interference to the hillside. Using 2x12 vertical rails anchored into the hill with 1-1/2 inch galvanized pipe, I then install the steps inside the rails. In reality I'm creating a ladder at any angle. Its always good to add a handrail for safety.

121

Nicholson Residence

Malibu

At the time, Jack was playing tennis with John McEnroe so he needed a tennis court. We not only designed the court but the entire property around the old ranch house. To get the water we needed we drilled a well and installed two 10,000 gallon water tanks. A big fire came through Malibu a few years later and burned everything except Jack's property. Not one tree was burned—not even the old Pines and Eucalyptus. The garden saved his house. These old trees hold a lot of water so they do not burn. When they are not watered, they fill up with oil and sap making them very drought tolerant, but a fire hazard. When they are watered, they become a reservoir full of water. Picture a paper cup filled with water and put it in a fire. It will not burn.

Whenever I work on properties in fire areas, I plant a lot of trees that hold a lot of water, such as Sycamores and Corals. These trees will divert a fire and quite often save your house.

Mayer Residence

Hidden Hills

These are all large horse properties and quite fun to work on. We
changed the entry with a long metal
hoop arbor covered in vines. In the
backyard I designed a raised wood
deck and arbor at the corner of the
court. Not the usual spot for a viewing terrace, however in this case
it worked for the court and garden
together.

Before

McVie Residence

Bell Canyon

A very steep hillside which turned out to be quite interesting. It was a great garden but quite expensive due to the massive retaining walls. To solve the problem, we covered the walls with artificial stone to make it look like natural rock.

Before

Moss Bodck Residence

Westwood

Since there was hardly any back yard, we enclosed the front yard to create the private space.

Licklider Residence

Bel Air

This was a hillside property on a flag lot. We curved the driveway and added lots of trees. We also enlarged the motor court area so a car could back up and turn around, and guest parking was added. In the back we re-designed the pool house to be underground with an open terrace on top to keep the open view. This gave me the opportunity to utilize the hillside and create a pathway from the front to the back through a forest of trees.

Before

Kuklin Residence
Studio City

A small horizon pool overlooking the valley with a pool house and bath. In the rear set back we created a secret garden for the kids. This was a no-mans-land that would have been unused. It is now a great play area for the kids. It includes a hiking path and a great little kitchen garden.

Before

133

Josephson Residence

Santa Monica

This property is a small Italian villa right on the beach. The date palms work great here and give an instant punch to the garden. The idea is to make the garden look like it's been there forever.

Before

135

Before

Goldring Residence

Pacific Palisades

The city would not allow me to add a second story to the garage so I raised the roof to 13 ft. and added bi-fold doors and turned it into a dance studio for the kids. I was also able to do a great sun deck on top. By designing doors that will allow a car into the space it remains a garage. For resale, this is important.

Before

Feinberg Residence

Pacific Palisades

This house had a very small intimate garden with water elements and an outdoor fireplace.

Before

Fourticq Residence

Hancock Park

This was an old-word house. It just needed a little charm. We created a canopy of trees over the driveway and separated the pedestrian entry with a rose garden.

Bright Residence

Mandeville Canyon

This was the second house I did for Kevin and Claudia. The kids were now older and asked for a basketball court. We lowered it 4 ft. into the ground so we only had a 4 ft. fence on top to look at. Play courts need an 8 ft. fence and tennis courts need a 10 ft. fence. By lowering the courts a minimum of 4 ft. you lessen the visual impact. It also makes the viewing better by looking down.

Barbee Residence
West Los Angeles

This was a Bird house which had been totally restored. Bird was an architect in the 50s that did these beautiful small craftsman houses. His son, Gary Bird, continued in this style and I continued working with him on several other projects.

Massman Residence

Brentwood

This was a very early project of mine. The back yard was very small and the neighbor's driveway was just 5 ft. behind the pool. The way the planting was done gave it depth and made the space feel much larger. That was the key.

Kramer Residence

Encino

A hillside property on a flag lot. The curved driveway made a huge difference. The rear garden terraced into the hill. I used artificial rock to hide all my retaining walls.

Before

Sunset Marquis Hotel

Hollywood

Located on the Sunset Strip, this hotel is famous for the many musicians who stay there—it has its own recording studio. It's an old hotel that George Rosenthal owned for many years before he was able to enlarge it with new villas backing up to La Cienega. He asked me to meet with his architects and engineers. The new villas were designed to be on top of two levels of garage so it would become a rooftop garden. I suggested lowering the garages 5 ft. and beefing up the structural slab to put 5 ft. of soil on top. There was dead silence, then laughter and then I was asked to leave. They hired someone else who designed the usual rooftop-type garden with raised planters and lots of pots. Months later, they fired their landscape architect and came back to me. I wasn't so crazy after all.

Now, as you walk through the garden villas, you have no idea that you are on top of a garage. People come here because of the gardens. Its an oasis in the city.

Griffin Towers

Newport Beach

These were two large red office buildings with a huge motor court in the middle. Way too much concrete. I mounded the center and added large palm trees with red begonias to match the building color and changed the concrete to a colored concrete with a pattern. I also reduced the diameter by adding a walking path around the outer edge, thus keeping fire code requirements.

Osher Residence

Santa Monica

I did his parent's house years earlier. When the grandkids come to me I know it's time to quit.

Recht Garden

Beverly Hills

By adding a false wall at the second story I was able to stretch the house and give it a more horizontal look. It is very important to always look at the architecture as well as the garden. Sometimes the solution to the garden has a direct connection to the architecture.

154

Hunt Pando Residence

Hollywood Hills

I was hired to create a small spa and garden off the master bedroom. By playing around with different ideas I was able to fit in a small pool and spa in a grotto with a sun deck above. The large retaining wall is notched for a stone bench on the upper deck. You feel that you are sitting on a small garden wall and not on top of a 10 ft retaining wall. Everything was layered up so you never felt the major grade change in such a small area.

Walder Residence

Malibu

This was a five year project sitting on 40 acres overlooking the ocean. In the end we ran out of money and he had to sell the house. He was able to live in it for a short period of time to fulfill his dream. He was a great guy.

Freeman Storage Units

Westlake

This was a very simple transformation. Unique signage with better landscaping and a change of building color. Commercial space doesn't have to look commercial.

Farkas Residence

West Los Angeles

Changing the entry position was the key that unlocked the magic here. Also curving the walk up to the house gave us more room to create landings and break up the long run of steps. It also made the property feel much larger. The right design will make the property feel ten times bigger.

Montgomery-Duban Wäechter Residence

Mar Vista

This was a project I did for the daughter of my accountant and friend Dennis Duban. She had just gotten married and this was their first house. We gave it a little better curb appeal.

Goldberg Residence

Brentwood

Pulling the motor court away from the house and creating a walkway through a garden gave the house more of an estate feel.

Arnopole Residence

Brentwood

We took a 60s house and turned it into a French country estate. We did a pool within a pool to save on permits and took away all the paving, walls and fences. We expanded the garden down the hill and made the property blend into the distant view.

TSA Drake Manor

Pomona

This was one of over 50 low-cost and senior housing projects that I did for Tom Safran Associates. He won awards on all of them. His big thing was landscaping. Landscaping is what makes people happy. This was his philosophy and he would give me free reign to make this happen. Quite often he would put his own money in to complete the landscaping if we were running out at the end.

TSA Breezewood

Whittier

This was another TSA project where I was able to work with the architect and site the buildings as well as designing the rest of the landscape. There are bridges with dry creek beds, a swimming pool, a putting green and a lush garden.

It was interesting that TSA was doing another similar project in Riverside at the same time with another architect and landscape architect. They approached it more conventionally and Tom was not happy. The other project ended up costing more and I was asked to go in and fix it. While doing this, I did a comparison study showing Tom why the other project cost more and came out not as good.

Moving the sidewalk, the planting area obscures the view to the parking lot.

Curving the walkway allows for more room for planting and better privacy.

Here is the analysis:

1) Buildings were not sited but laid out in a grid;

2) Too much concrete also done in straight lines;

3) Bigger box trees were specified but not tagged;

4) Fancy iron work was designed and then covered in vines or hedges.

All in all they did not get much bang for their buck. Tom did not use them again. It was a good lesson in the fact that good design is very economical and a good designer spends the money where it counts.

A simple arbor visually enlarges the space and creates a transition through the garden.

TSA Hancock Gardens

Hancock Park

This was a low-cost senior housing project with a high percentage of Asian residents. I included a large garden area with individual plots plus a great garden with walking paths and sitting areas. I included a large open grass area for Tai Chi. Good gardens do make people happy.

After 35 years and over 50 award-winning projects, Tom Safran retired and turned the reins over to younger people. At this point, my gardens were costing more than was required for low-cost housing. As a result other landscape architects were brought in to take over at a lesser cost and greater profit margin for TSA.

I would often go back to check on my gardens to make sure they were being maintained properly. I trained the tree trimmers and gardeners to take care of the gardens correctly. No blowing or shaping the shrubs and trees, etc. Proper maintenance makes a huge difference.

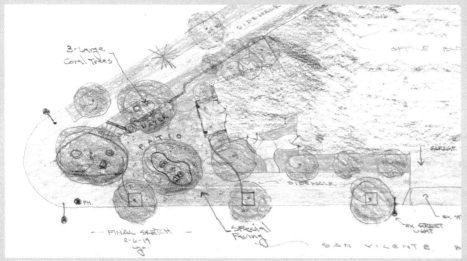

TSA Office Building

Brentwood

When Tom hired Frank Gehry to design his office building the one stipulation was that he had to have me do the landscape. This is one of the few Frank Gehry buildings that you will see with landscaping surrounding the building instead of concrete. My goal was to make the building feel that it was emerging from the trees around it. Rather than standing out, it would blend into the environment. Site takes precedence over the architecture.

This is one project I did not oversee and a few mistakes happened. Two major Coral trees were eliminated and my paving pattern was not extended to the curb as per my design.

Frank told me I should be an architect instead of a landscape architect. I told him that I prefer being a landscape architect. I find it more challenging and more rewarding in the end. I find that good landscape architecture can even make bad architecture look good.

Falkenberg Solt Residence
Rancho Boa Vista

Santa Barbara

This is a beautiful 50-acre property high in the hills of Solvang with amazing views and old oak trees. The house and gardens were designed around these beautiful trees. The challenge here was to design around the existing oaks.

Andrew and Claudia have a vineyard and an olive grove where they produce their own wine and olive oil which makes it quite special.

173

Simpson Residence

San Moreno

The garage was in the back yard
facing the pool and patio. By adding
an arbor it softened the focus of the
garage doors.

Another good solution is using glass
doors that will act as a mirror and
reflect the garden.

Witt Residence

Westlake Village

We designed a very natural garden to blend with the surrounding nature. The idea is to make it look as if it has been there forever and was never designed. My wooden bridge gave me the transition from gravel to stone. I leave the timbers loose to create a rumbling sound. Sound is an important part of the garden. You can find this in the sound of water, the rustling of leaves, the sounds of animals, etc.

Before

177

Wagner Residence

Hollywood

A very simple house built in the 60s that we turned into a modern gem. We took out the circular drive and enclosed a private entry with a koi pond and bridge to a glass front door that looked through to the small backyard and pool.

Over the years I have experimented with various color combinations that will determine the color of the water in the pool. For example, a tan plaster gives the water a mediterranean look while a gray plaster will be a blue color. The darker the shade of gray, the darker the blue. I personally like a mixture of gray and green plaster which gives the water a beautiful blue with a touch of green. Delightful to swim in. I also match the tile to the water color. I use a plain tile that will disappear—you want your eye to focus on the entire garden, not just the tile.

179

Tunney Residence

Malibu

John and Katinka were one of the few clients that hired me to develop the site before they hired an architect. I laid out the building, entry and parking plus pool and pool house sites. The key was not allowing the house to dominate the site.

By keeping the site primary, I was able to design all the elements to fit into the overall site. Back to primary and secondary space relationships. The site should always be considered primary whenever possible.

Before

Valero Residence

Hidden Hills

We gave this property a Palm Beach look. You feel like you are in Florida.

Hawn Russell Residence

Pacific Palisades

This was the second house I did for Goldie when she was with Kurt Russell. It had a pool and a sunken play court and a great garden.

186

Weil Residence

Brentwood

This was an early project of mine. I rotated the garage to create a separate and private motor court that did not face the front door as the architect designed. This gave me the ability to create a primary pedestrian entry. Very elegant and very old world. In the backyard we were going to do a natural pool when at the last minute Marty and Ruth asked if we could do a koi pond instead. Instead of a plaster pool which would kill the fish we thoro-sealed the shell and did a sand filter. This would allow us to turn it back into a pool anytime.

Several years later they had a young couple living in the back guest house that had a baby. They told me one day they were sorry there wasn't a pool. I suggested they get in and swim with the fish, so they did. The baby loved it and so did the fish, they would all swim back and forth together. I learned here how smart and social koi really are. More people should do this.

187

Salomon Residence

Hollywood Hills

This property had great views but a bad entry with a large retaining wall. To break it up I created pockets of artificial rock outcroppings with hedge and vines in-between. At the entry we planted several large specimen olive trees and a rock waterfall. You would never believe this all hid a 12 ft. retaining wall.

Doughterty Dirks Residence
Bel Air

There are properties in the hills that have a lot of land the owners think is wasted space. Not so! It is amazing what can be done with a hillside.

I love using old broken concrete to create my garden terrace walls—much better for a natural look. It also allows moisture to bleed through eliminating the hydrostatic pressure that you get behind a regular block retaining wall. By keeping the height of the walls low and doing multiple terraces you are able to create a much more natural look.

Danley Residence
Beverly Hills

When we finished this property the owner rented the house to Prince. He loved it and stayed here for many years.

We designed this house and garden to look like an old Italian villa.

Nahai Residence

Beverly Hills

This was an early job where I included dinners as part of my fee. Eating in those days was a big priority. The kids were about 10 years old at the time so I got to watch them grow up. One night at dinner years later when the daughter, Oz as I call her, was in her early 30s, I asked Mahnaz if she would mind if I asked her daughter out. She looked at me and said, "If you do that there will be no more dinners." I kept the dinners. Today both kids are married with their own kids. I have done both of their gardens. I guess I am the honorary uncle. I think the little one likes me.

Before

Nahai Residence
Santa Monica

Shahrad was ten years old when I designed the garden for his parents. He is now married to his beautiful wife, Tania. This is their first house. It was built by a developer with not much thought put into the gardens. The main problem was the entry— straight in to the front door. This cut the space in half and took away all privacy. By coming in from the corner, we were able to give much better privacy and make the space feel larger. Since the front yard faces west, they now are able to sit there in the late afternoon with a glass of wine. It is now a usable space which most front yards are not.

Why does everyone paint their perimeter walls and fences white? Light colors come forward making a space feel smaller while dark colors go away making a space feel bigger. I paint most of my walls and fences Boxwood Green by Sherman Williams. It blends with the plant material and makes borders disappear.

Wollons Residence

Hidden Hills

The client just installed a pool then came to me to design the garden. I told them the pool was in the wrong place. We took it out and re-designed the garden. I designed a new pool up the hill along with a paddle tennis court. This took advantage of a much better view and lots of sun. I did keep the spa since it was a separate unit and tied it into a stream and pond.

Again, the site design is the most important part of the landscape. Organization of space is the key.

Abdul Jabbar Residence

Bel Air

This started out as a large two story Italian villa that the Bel Air architectural committee would not approve. Their reason was that it was too big and right on Stone Canyon Drive. The house was on a corner lot. I turned the house on a 45-degree angle to the corner so you only saw the corners of the house from the street. This eliminated the front yard, side yard and rear yard and gave me the opportunity to wrap gardens all the way around without any divisions.

I was also able to design an underground gym with a racquet ball court in the back. I remember Kareem asking the architect, "Can he do this?" With my re-design, the Bel Air committee then approved it and we built it. With the pool, Kareem told me to make sure it was long enough for him. We made it 70 ft. long..

Norian Residence
Beverly Hills

This was an old house in an old neighborhood. We injected a little charm which made it special. It is always important to not over-design a space. You want the character of the house to fit into the neighborhood. When done, it should look as if it has always been there.

Before

203

Freeman Residence
Sherman Oaks

Glenn and I play racquetball together so this was a fun project. In the backyard I needed an arbor but did not want posts in the patio. I used a steel 4x6 inch tubular beam to span 35 ft. to hang my wood beams off of. It gives the appearance of a floating arbor. I am starting to use more and more steel in my designs these days. You get much greater spans allowing you to eliminate vertical posts that tend to break up the space making the garden feel smaller.

Before

Elins Residence

Encino

This was a large estate up in the hills. We did a paddle tennis court plus pool and ponds. We also got a great circular drive in a space that was very tight against the street. A forest of Redwoods did the trick.

At the end of the project Larry gave me a bonus check that was greater than my entire fee. I am still shocked!

Murrell Residence

Santa Monica

This was a small house in the flats of Santa Monica. This was a very small space to work with but it had the most amazing feeling when we finished. There is a lot of magic to be found in small spaces.

They sold the house to a single man who bought it for the garden. When he first looked at the house he told his real estate agent to go away and come back in an hour. He sat and meditated in the garden. When she came back he said I want it. He bought it for full price allowing my clients, John and Sheila, to move to North Carolina to start their business and family.

They had two twin boys, Christopher and Garrett born one day after my birthday. Garrett was named after me and is quite different from his brother. He not only looks like me but has the same interests and oddities. They are now in their 20s. It has been interesting watching them grow up.

Pietsch Wilson Residence

Studio City

Marilyn and Scooter got married in Hawaii and wanted a Hawaiian-style garden. My friend Aviva and I had just returned from Bali so that had a big influence on my design.

Before

211

Ketchum Residence
Beverly Hills

Stuart was a great guy—one of the early surfers. He was the builder who built Disney Hall. He wanted his garden to look like an old Italian villa. We used a lot of old olives and Italian cypress with red fescue grass and wildflowers. The front was very wild and the back was very tailored.

213

Before

Phoenix dactylifera

Hirsch Residence

Agoura Hills

This was the first time I used the date palm from Palm Springs—Phoenix dactylifera. Richard and Diana owned property in Palm Springs where they were going to build a shopping center. The property was a date palm grove. They were going to cut all of them down! I convinced Richard to try some in his garden to see if they would survive.

They not only survived but did great!

I started using them everywhere. They are able to take hot and cold and did great right on the beach. It's funny they were not commonly used in an ornamental application. Now you see them everywhere. In the beginning I got them for free, just digging and transport cost. Now they cost around $2,500—about the same cost as an olive tree. Both are easy to transplant and give you big bang for your buck. I also did a ski house for them in Deer Valley.

Hubner Residence

Trousdale Estates

I worked with Hal Levitt on this project. Hal added on to the house in a circular fashion. I was then able to tie on to his archiecture and fully enclose the motor court. In the back it had an existing pool with a large concrete patio with a 4 ft. hedge at the top of the slope. All of this blocked your down view into the city. I notched the bond beam of the pool and added a pond 18 inches lower. By lowering the existing grade I was able to achieve a fabulous down view into the city.

About 10 years ago someone knocked on his door and wanted to buy his house. "Name the price!" Three times higher than the highest selling house in Trousdale at that time was Bill's response. He did not want to sell the house. The kid brought his client who pulled out his checkbook and wrote Bill a check for the full amount, and asked if he could be out in 30 days. Bill took it and was out in 30 days.

Rogers Residence
Calabasas

This was a large piece of property where we put in a pool and sunken play court. It had great views to the surrounding hills. We used a lot of palms and olives. A nice combination that does well in hot and dry areas.

Before

219

Heller Residence

Brentwood

Nancy loved to flip houses. She was quite good at it. This one was a 70s house that we turned into a very modern house. I took out the old pool which took up the entire center of the garden and re-designed a new modern pool off to the side leaving the center open for view and play. Once again making the site primary and the pool secondary. I also opened up the hillside which was fenced off before.

Before

221

Before

222

Kenny Residence

Outpost Drive
Hollywood Hills

Doug was a great guy who came to Hollywood out of Harvard. He helped start National Lampoon and wrote the movies Animal House and Caddyshack.

This was an impossible job that people said could not be done. Everything was terraced into the hill with no wall over 4 ft. in height. It was all done by hand and took over a year to do.

He and I were the same age at the time—34. Just before the job finished, while he was in Hawaii, he died. Sadly, he never got to swim in the pool.

I miss Doug, he was one of a kind.

Before

Kaplan Residence

Toluca Lake

This was a new house which we made to look old-world. The entry had a small fountain with a gravel path leading to the front door. We also did a wild mix of planting with lots of color.

225

Kamm Residence

Encino

This was a small backyard with a lot of grade change. By using a series of terraces we were able to connect the house and garden in a much better way.

Sonny and Gloria have one of the largest teapot collections in the world. It travels to shows and museums internationally and is really something to see.

Before

228

Klee Residence

Brentwood

This was a transformation that even surprised me. Getting rid of the straight lines was the main key in finding the magic. It has an energy now that was missing before.

Before

229

230

Lidow Residence

Santa Monica Canyon

I was able to save a big Sycamore tree by convincing the architect to design the building with the tree going through the roof. The property had lots of big trees. You always need to learn to work with what you have—very important!

Beverly Park Estate
Beverly Hills

This was a 5-acre property where half of it was unused—totally dead space. The entry came into the front door with a very small motor court that could barely hold 4 cars. The rose garden was a series of terrace walls going up the hill and hard to access. The key to making the property work was changing the entry.

We took this negative wasted space and turned it into a long entry approach to the house. We got a much better motor court and total privacy from the street. The rose garden became our koi pond without any retaining walls showing. The trick is taking negative space and turning it into positive space.

233

234

Mayer Residence
Santa Monica Canyon

John is a great mountain bike rider so we had a lot in common. His property is right next door to the Lidow property and the feeling is quite similar.

Before

Before

After

Levine Residence

Beverly Hills

The transformation on this property was like night and day. The character of the house totally changed and thus so did the garden.

Note the side yard. I find these small spaces very important and treat them in a special way.

237

Klein Residence

Santa Monica Canyon

This was a new house on a very tight lot. We had a series of very small pocket spaces to work with. The key to making the property work was connecting the house to the garden with big openings. Also, heavy planting was the key to making the site feel bigger.

Einstein Residence

Brentwood

This was a very modern house filled with all their old-world furniture. I thought they needed to modernize the inside as well—throw all this old stuff out. So they did! This got them on the road to collecting modern art and changed their lives.

I never wore a watch in those days and was always late so Cliff gave me my first watch—a Porsche watch which I still own. These days I try to always be on time.

Their property had very little space to work with so we ended up putting the pool in the side yard and extending it out into the front yard. We had a great piece of sculpture at the end which you would see as you walked to the front door. Another example of turning negative space into positive space.

241

Beverly Hills

Santa Barbara

Fletcher Residence

Beverly Hills and Santa Barbara

Jane and Seymour were neighbors in the 80s and were remodeling an old Spanish house down the street. Every day I would drive by and wonder what they were doing. One day I stopped and offered my help—for free. I re-designed the house to fit into the hillside better by creating small terraces from the different levels of the house as it stepped up the hill. These terraces then worked their way down to a lap pool at the bottom. Fitting the house to the hill was the trick that made it work.

Several years later, they sold the house, bought 40 acres in Santa Barbara and hired me to create a complete site plan. They hired a local architect to do the building in a Spanish style. The architect designed the house at the existing grade with large cantilevered decks hanging off the back looking out to the ocean. I suggested they lower the house 8 ft. into the hill and push the soil down to create a garden. This allowed the house to exit on grade which was a better solution. The entrance was better as well since when you drive up you don't see a big house. Instead, you see the view over the roof—beautiful! The architect was furious but Jane, who was a set designer, saw the advantage right away and went with it. The key here was the grading which allowed us to maximize a larger portion of the site. Seymour walks the property every day and rarely leaves. Who can blame him?

243

244

Rock from the property was used to create rubble walls

245

246

Lawson Residence

Santa Monica Canyon

I had just returned from a trip to San Miguel de Allende in Mexico. The colors they use are incredible so I borrowed a few ideas. Never be afraid to borrow.

Personal Projects

Westcliffe, Colorado

View from the main house

In 1990 I had two offices. LandArc, which I started in 1975, was doing mostly high-end residential work and CMA (Carlson, Melendrez and Associates) was doing mostly commercial projects. CMA was started in 1985 and took 3 or 4 years to build up. In reality, I did this as a favor to my school friend Lauren Melendrez. She was tired of working for a large firm (POD) at the time. By having her own firm, it gave her more money and time to raise her daughter. She loved the commercial work—I hated it!

At this point in my life I needed a change, so one day I walked into the office and gave CMA to Lauren as a gift. She took the office and increased the staff up to around 25 and moved it to downtown LA. I took my LandArc office which was usually between 3 and 5 people and started hand-picking my clients. I would work 70% and play 30%.

Site Plan

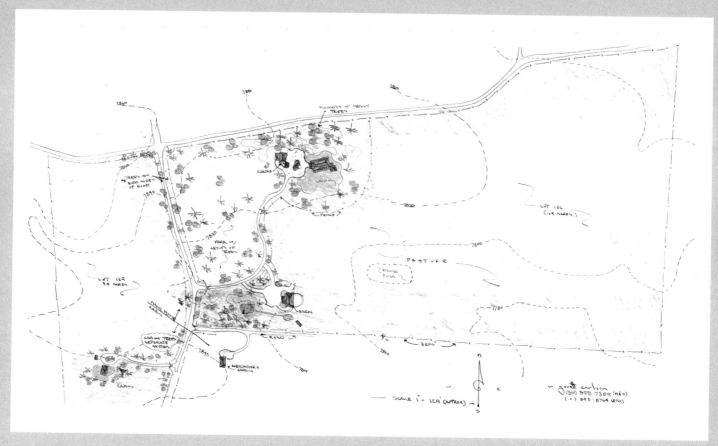

My first cabin

The Ranch

Colorado

At this time I went to Colorado and bought 150 acres on a prairie with great views but no trees. I built a little cabin and promised myself to go there once a month for a minimum of five or six days. I have been good to my word for thirty years now. I used this time to relax and decompress from Los Angeles.

I spent ten to fifteen years developing my ranch. I built a barn, a pond with a windmill and then a main house. The main house took three years to build and three years to furnish.

Main Ranch House

Frosty, one of my horses

I planted two to three thousand trees. I planted most of them myself with one helper. They started out at about three to five ft. tall.

It's nice to watch things grow.

255

The Feed Store

Colorado

A few years after I bought the 150 acres I bought an old building in the town of Westcliffe. Built in the 1880s, it had been abandoned for many years and was really a tear-down. I spent six years restoring it back to its original condition. It was the original feed store for the town. The building was jacked up to create a basement with a micro-brew below, a restaurant on the first floor, two apartments on the second floor and a penthouse apartment on the third floor.

I bought an acre behind the building and created a park, an underground amphitheater and planted over a thousand trees. We had an outdoor saloon, a miner's cabin and hiking paths all through the park. This started the Summer in the Park program.

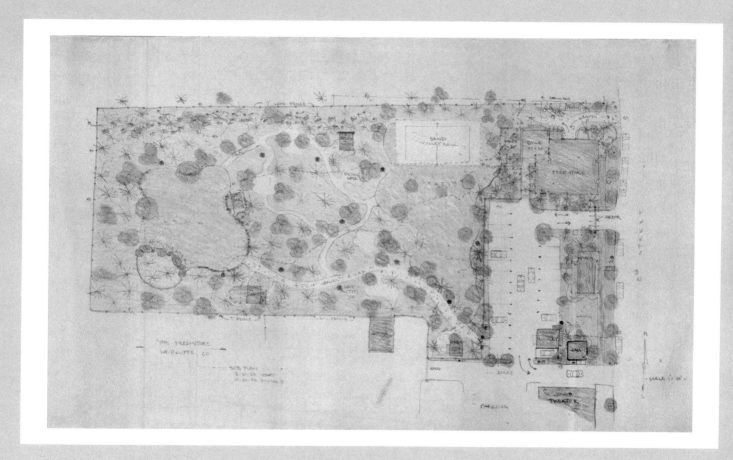

There were free concerts on Sundays, three weeks of Shakespeare plays, a kid's jazz camp, Easter egg hunts, weddings and private parties. This became a large part of the community.

I wrote a history of the Feed Store from its beginning. Very interesting, especially the ghosts.

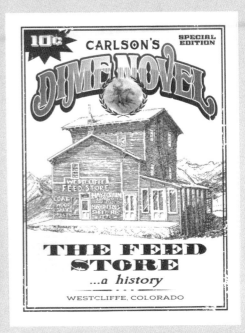

Boulder House

Joshua Tree

In 2008, I created another diversion in my life by starting to do more of my own projects, including more architecture. This allowed me to not only design the site and gardens but the buildings as well and gave me full control of a project—allowing for greater overall design.

I discovered Joshua Tree in the California desert while doing a bike ride. It was a small town with lots of artists and a great vibe. I bought several lots in one isolated area with the idea of doing a small community of unusual houses.

The project was on 5 acres. It was an interesting house with a sod roof and heated and cooled floors. Half the house was covered in artificial rock to protect it from the heat. Gilbert, my rock guy, created all this. People think this is natural rock and wonder how the house was built around them. The other end was all glass that disappeared into side pockets allowing for uninterrupted views to the valley below.

The house was featured on *HGTV Extreme Homes* and written up in several architectural magazines. We planted over 450 desert trees and over a thousand shrubs. Today it is a habitat for several red tail hawks and several other types of birds and wildlife.

It was an interesting project so I put together a small book, *Building the Boulder House*.

Site Plan

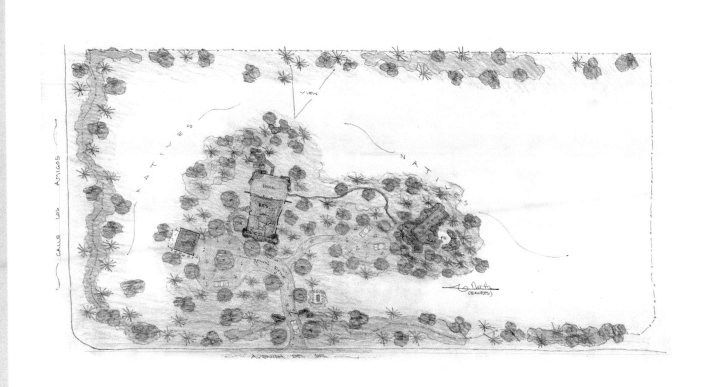

After selling the house, the new owner asked me to design a swimming pool. It's a bit of an unusual pool but was designed to fit the character of the house.

Gilbert came back again to create some more of his amazing rock work.

265

Desert Horizon House

Joshua Tree

This is my second house in Joshua Tree. It is just the opposite from the Boulder House—very modern with big overhanging roofs and lots of glass. It sits across the street on 3 acres.

My next house will be two lots away on 3 acres as well. It will be a floating house in three parts over a dry lake bed. To go to your bedroom you will need to go outside on a raised catwalk under the stars. The idea is to experience nature.

And, if I survive this house, my next one will be one street back on a 6-acre piece of property. It will be an underground house totally off the grid. I will still have two more 3-acre lots to play with.

267

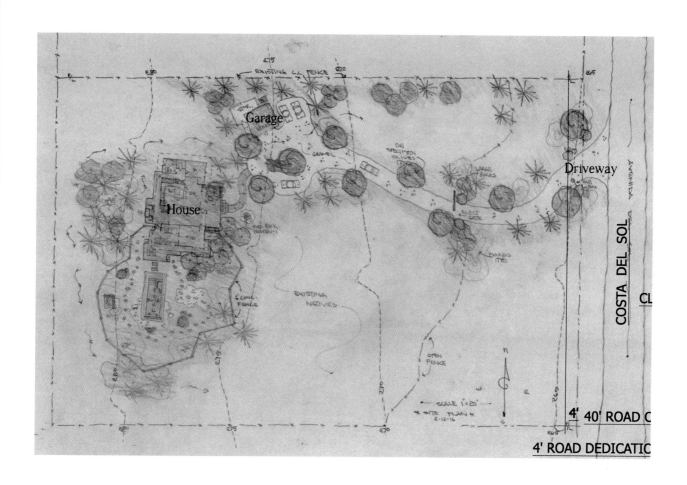

269

Rough Concept Sketch

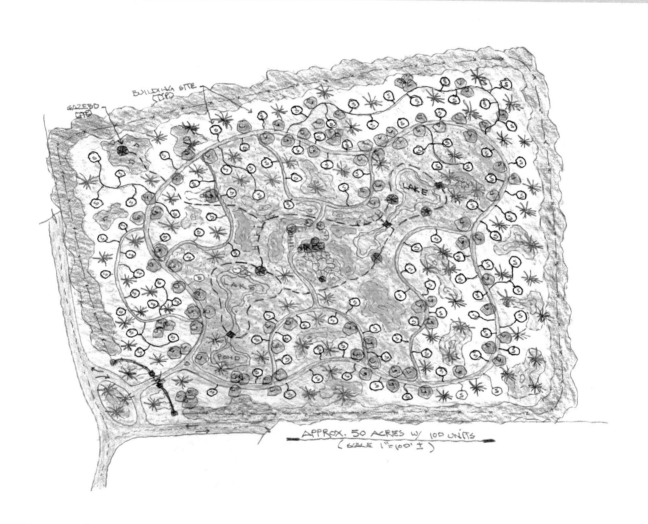

Small Communities

One last project I would still like to do is what I call my manufactured home park. A low density community of 50-100 small pre-fab houses of 800-1500 sq. ft. each. The houses would be set in a 25-50 acre site with no property boundaries. Set at different angles, each house would have a small secure backyard.

Selling for a modest amount of money, they would be be designed for young people starting out with young families and older people downsizing. The developer would own the property and charge a home owners fee for the mainte-nance of the park. It would have a 24-hour guard, a central club house, plus hiking paths and perhaps a lake or two with fish for the kids to catch.

These small communities would be located within an hour of a big city with an airport and hospital in an area with a good climate. With the amount of baby boomers these days and young people trying to get started I think these communities would be a big success.

Concrete Channel

Lower Benedict Canyon

THE POTS: In the 60s the city installed a storm channel on lower Benedict Canyon. To minimize the eyesore they placed 60 pots along this 600 ft. stretch. They were never maintained and always looked bad. In 1990 there was a trash truck accident that broke the irrigation line that ran along the fence. The city shut the water off and was waiting to let everything die so they could get rid of the pots. No one would take any responsibility—I decided to step in. Over 4,000 cars drive by every day and I drive by at least 4 times myself. I fixed the irrigation and started to replant the pots.

On Sundays, my friend Catherine and I would add to the planting. After a few years the Benedict Canyon Association discovered that it was me and came to my rescue with a grant to re-do all the planting and put in a better irrigation system. The pots are getting quite old and more difficult to keep alive—I lose a few every year.

The advantage of the pots is that they make people smile as they drive by— helping to put a little joy in everyone's life. Without the pots you would be looking at an empty concrete channel. Beauty goes a long way.

Upper Benedict Canyon

Just recently we did the same thing at the top of Benedict Canyon. With the help of a great neighbor and Mindy, a good friend and an old client, we got lots of cuttings given to us by different people. With these and some small native trees we did a very nice dry garden. It doesn't look like much now but it will in a year or two. Hopefully this will get a smile at both ends of the canyon.

273

The Team

276

It's Always a Team Project

I have been very fortunate in my career to have worked with some of the finest contractors in the business. They have helped me make my designs better through their knowledge and experience. I always ask them what they think and how we can make it better together. When they are involved, they have more ownership. Quite often I find some of the workers bringing their families back to a finished project to show it off. It is important to build a team of people that you can trust and can accomplish what you envision.

My favorite pool contractor was Archie Kapp. He did most of my crazy pools.

Gerardo Avilucea—Gilbert the rock guy— is a true artist with artificial rock. You have seen his work thoughout the book. There are very few that can make rock look so real.

There are two landscape contractors I have worked with for over 30 years. The first is Jason Sanders of Harold Jones. His main foreman, Raul Sandoval is the main person I work with in the field. He can do anything and nothing is ever a problem. The other firm is Clark and White—Jim Clark and Dana White. Dana worked in my CMA office and I put her together with Jim many years ago. I work mostly with Jim and his great crew.

My tree broker is Claudia Calligari. I met her with Dudley in 1975. We always had fun taking clients to nurseries. She and her husband Bob have now retired and are traveling all over the world.

Bag of Tricks

There are so many things that I have learned along the way that I no longer really think about them as I design. In class the kids tell me to write them down.

So here goes:

1) The most important thing with a design is to keep the site primary and all the elements secondary. You want the eye to keep moving and not stop on any one item. This will create a sense of a much larger space, which is one of my primary goals.

2) Try to eliminate as many straight lines as possible both in the hardscape as well as the landscape. For instance, when trimming a hedge I will undulate the top rather than trimming it in a straight line. This allows the eye to travel through to the sky above creating pocket views. Also I will mix the plant material in a hedge so it's not all one type of plant. Try planting ficus and podocarpus together and perhaps add a few vines. This will take away the wall-like effect. When doing a fence, never put a top rail on it. Next time you see a chain link fence check to see if has a top rail or not. With a top rail, your eye stops. Without a rail, it goes right on through. I usually do a black chain link without a top rail and then plant it out. It disappears! Why spend money on something you don't want to see?

3) Borrow as much scenery as you can. Check out what's in the distance and add it to your site if possible. For instance, if there is a certain tree in the distance add one or more to your design. This allows the eye to connect the spaces thus making your space feel bigger.

4) Softscape is less expensive than hardscape so keep the hardscape to a minimum. I always try for 1/3 hardscape and 2/3 softscape. You get more energy out of landscape, especially trees.

5) Lay out everything in the field, this is very important. No matter how good the drawings are they are still just a guide. The final design will be 30% better with good field observation. This means from the beginning to the very end—you need to be there.

6) Always think about money. The better the design the more economical it is. For example, instead of doing a large retaining wall, perhaps a series of small rubble walls will work just as well. Less structure and more landscape for the eye to see. Way more bang for your buck. Your client will appreciate this, trust me.

7) Color in the garden. With walls and fences I try to paint them out with a color that blends with the planting. With plant material I will use more whites

in the foreground and darker colors like blues and purples in the background. This will give you greater depth in the garden.

8) Hand tagging your specimen trees not only saves money but gives you the ability to add character to the project. I always like bringing the client since this gets them involved and usually gets you a free lunch. The cost of a tree is based on the size of the container, so the bigger the tree in a smaller container saves you money. Instead of getting a 48 in. box tree maybe you could get three 24 in. box trees for the same money. I would quite often change my tree plan depending on what I found in the nursery. Once again, the plan is only a guide. These little changes will make the final outccome 30% better.

9) How to make a garden feel like it's been there forever and was never designed? That's a tough one. Don't make it too perfect. Use different size plants to get staggered heights. For instance if you are planting five Liquidambar trees, use a mix of sizes—perhaps one 36 in. box, two 24 in. box and two 15 gallon.

10) Learn what plants look good together and how to mix them to make them look natural. This has a lot to do with layering a garden. Start with large foundation trees and work your way down to the small material.

11) Art in the garden such as fountains, sculpture, benches, etc. make a statement.

12) Lighting is a must. Over the years I have developed my own special way of lighting a garden. Today I use all LED lighting. I use soft warm lights on the ground and cold white lights in the large trees as down lights to create a moonlight effect with great shadows. The planting plan usually dictates the lighting plan. When the planting plan changes so should your lighting plan.

13) Grading is important. A little bit of mounding will make a site feel bigger and also help drainage.

14) In any small space, designing on a diagonal will give the illusion of more space.

15) Materials are critical. Keep them as simple as possible. I use a lot of washed concrete with color in most of my large areas like driveways and big walkways. I tend to use natural stone in smaller, more intimate areas.

16) The most important thing of all is to travel the world and look at everything. Nothing is new, it has all been done before. It is how you put it all together that makes it unique, which is what makes your own design special.

To My Students

I think the future landscape architect will be more involved with habitat design not only for humans but more so for our animals and plants. I feel the animals and plants will contribute greatly to the health of our planet. Taking care of them will be a priority to ensure the continuation of us all. The spaces we live in are very important to our health and happiness. From small gardens to our large open spaces landscape architecture will always play a key role in how we live and interact in our environment.

There are a few ideas I have that would change our landscape dramatically.

Power lines should be underground or protected in a way to eliminate massive destructive tree trimming.

My next idea is more long range and has to do with getting rid of cars and providing more underground environments. If cities would require more underground parking it would change the balance of our open spaces.

Can you imagine a large shopping center totally underground where the entire surface area is a park?

I feel that designing underground will not only become a necessity in the future but a great challenge for the new landscape architect. I have a few ideas for underground houses that I still hope to do in the desert.

— W. Garett Carlson, ASLA

INDEX

Made in the USA
Middletown, DE
23 September 2020